SUPER DUPER DOODLES

DOODLES by:

_____

Publications International, Ltd.

Doodle yourself on the day you start this book.

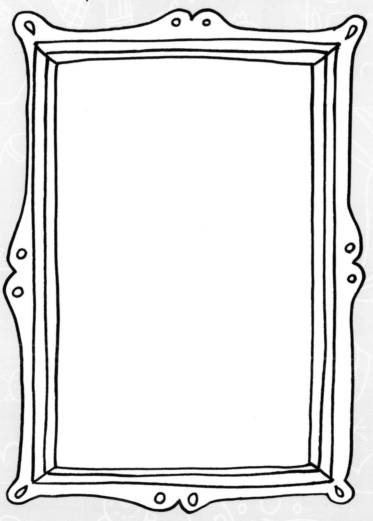

I started this book on: _____

Doodle Something FUN.

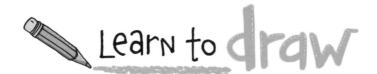

Learn to draw

Monkey

Hippo

Finish the doodles by adding detail and color.

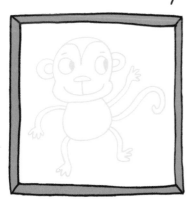

MAKE NEW FRIENDS!
doodle features on these faces.

GOING DOWN!

Doodle a parachute for the skydiver.

SLEEP TIGHT!
What are they dreaming?

Ladies and Gentlemen, I now present...

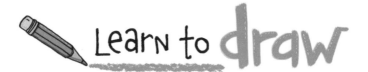

Learn to draw

Outer Space

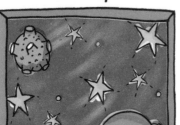

Alien

Finish the doodles by adding detail and color.

DOODLE SOMETHING BORING.

Turn these colorful shapes into your own creations.

say cheese! doodle your friends.

doodle your pets.

DOODLE FRAMES

finish the patterns, and doodle inside the frames.

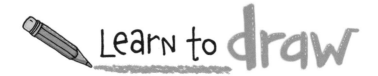

Learn to draw

Octopus

Submarine

Finish the doodles by adding detail and color.

Doodle a...

MONSTER

Doodle a flying machine.

DOODLE YOUR OWN MONSTER TRUCK.

CAREFUL, WE'RE HOT!
Doodle faces on these tasty snacks.

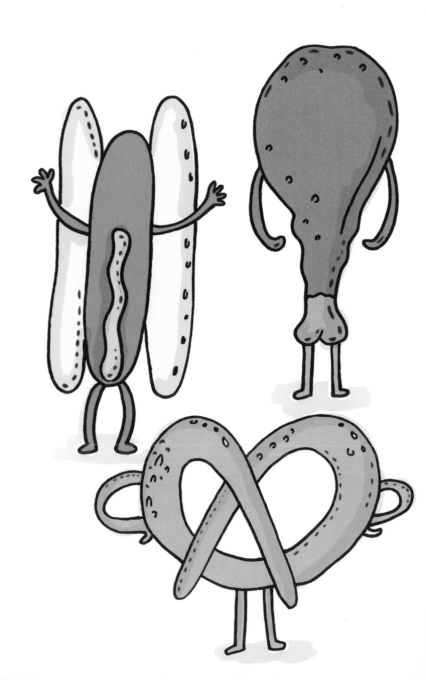

CONGRATULATIONS!

Doodle what you won.

welcome to the jungle! Doodle a wild scene.

MWA-HA-HA!

Doodle this mad scientist's invention.

Doodle a **PARTY!**

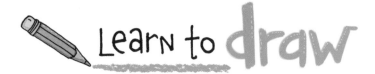
Learn to draw

microphone

keyboard

Finish the doodles by adding detail and color.

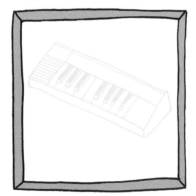

DOODLE SOMETHING

POINTY.

you've reached the
☆ OUTER LIMITS! ☆
what lives on this planet?

WILD THINGS!
Doodle faces on these furry friends.

catch some air, Dude!

DOODLE FRAMES

Finish the patterns, and doodle inside the frames.

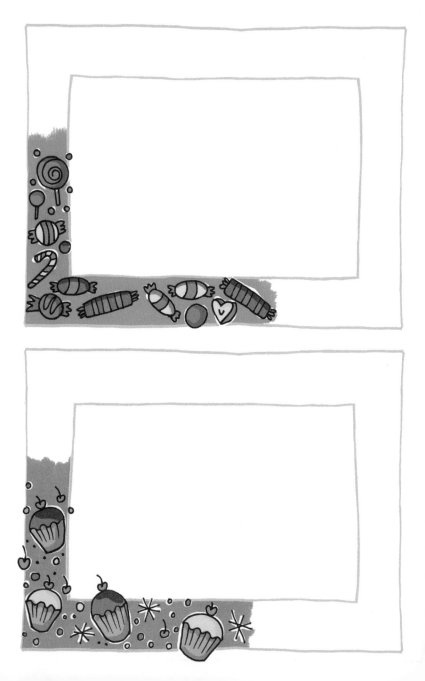

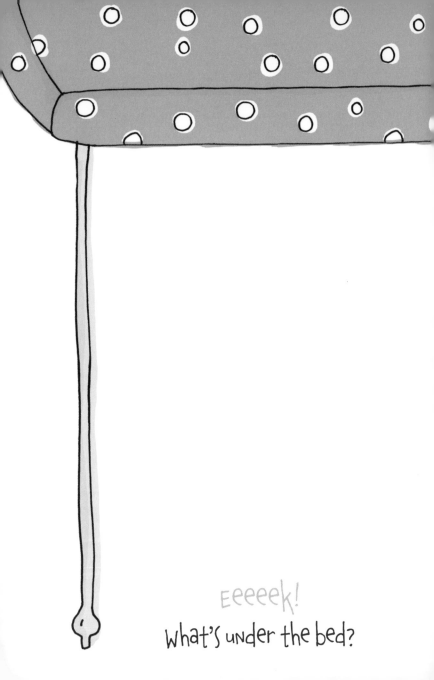

EEEEEK!
What's under the bed?

Doodle a... cartoon character

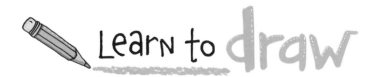 Learn to draw

Owl

Giraffe

Finish the doodles by adding detail and color.

smells good. what's for breakfast?

Eat up! What's for lunch?

SWEET! What's for dessert?

What do you see in the
deep blue sea?

DOODLE A...
SUPERHERO

doodle a...

VILLAIN

Doodle the yummiest sandwich.

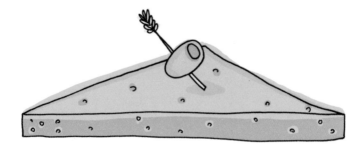

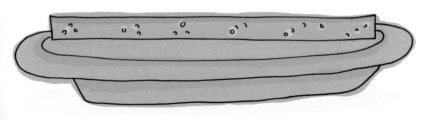

Doodle the weirdest sandwich.

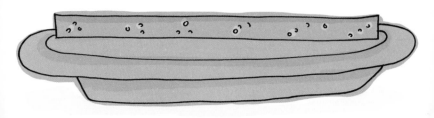

Argh! X marks the spot, matey.
Doodle a treasure map.

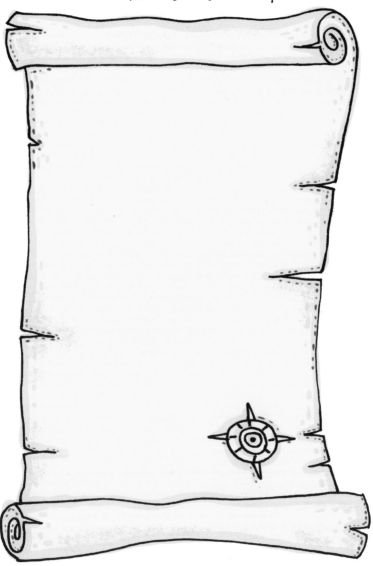

Blimey, you've found the booty!
Doodle the treasure.

GREETINGS, EARTHLINGS!
Add faces to these intergalactic creatures.

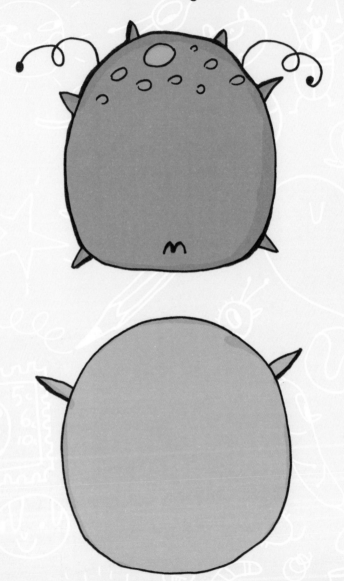

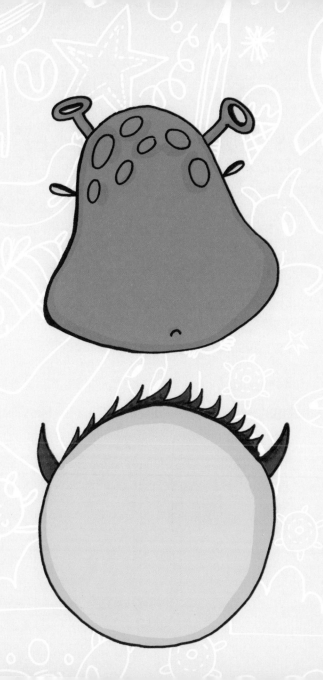

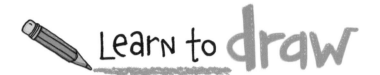

Astronaut

Rocket

Finish the doodles by adding detail and color.

DOODLE SOMETHING
Scary.

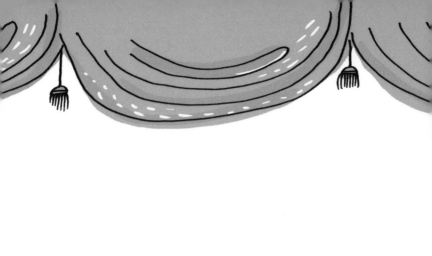

shhh! Doodle what's playing.

Doodle everything you can think of that's... **red.**

Hop to it!

YUM!

Add faces to these sweet treats.

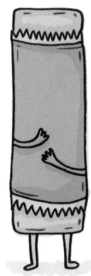

doodle something

silly

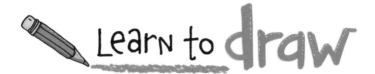

Learn to draw

Guitar

Drum

Finish the doodles by adding detail and color.

PACK IT UP!
Doodle what you need for school.

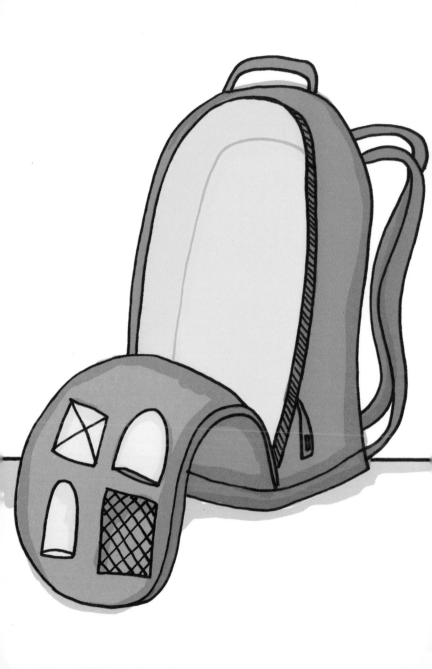

Doodle a family crest.

Doodle a royal crest.

color in the
DOODLE FOOD!

GET TO CLASS!

Doodle what's in these lockers.

PACK YOUR LUNCH!

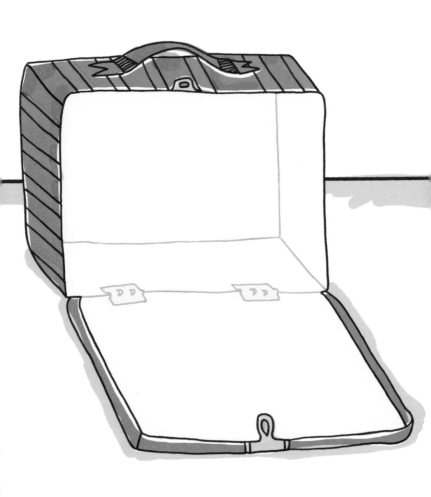

Doodle everything you can think of that's... blue.

PRECIOUS PETS
Add faces to these animals.

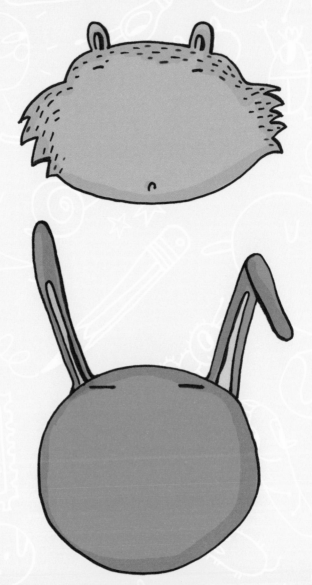

WHEEE!

Finish the roller coaster.

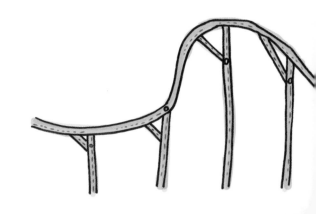

Strike a pose!

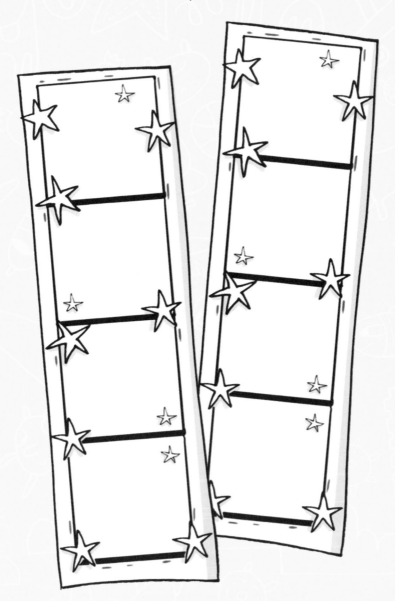

Doodle your favorite celebrities.

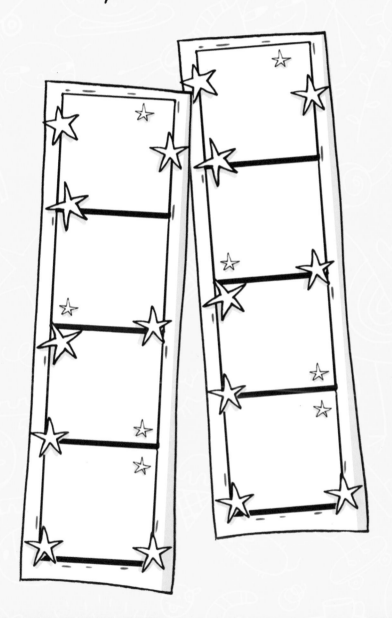

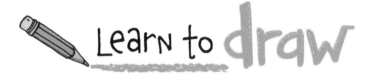 Learn to draw

Helicopter

Scooter

Finish the doodles by adding detail and color.

DOODLE SOMETHING BOLD.

Turn these colorful shapes into your own creations.

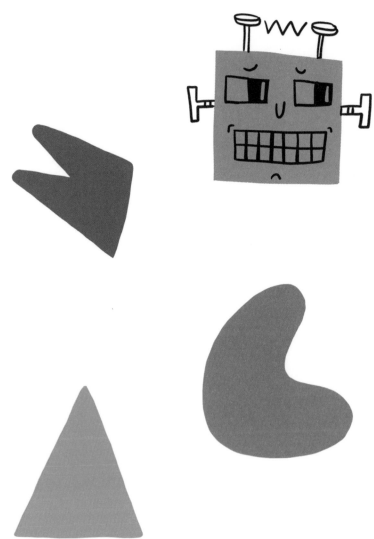

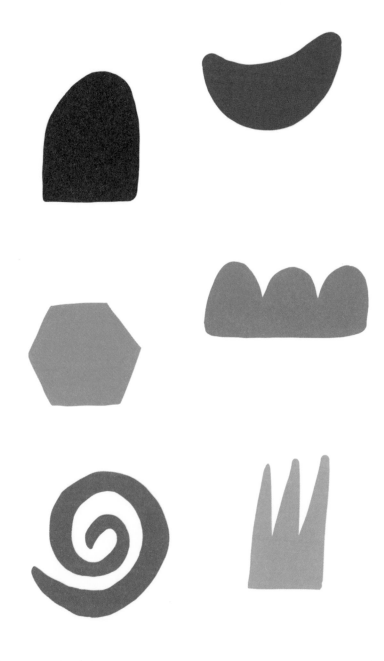

What's in the room?

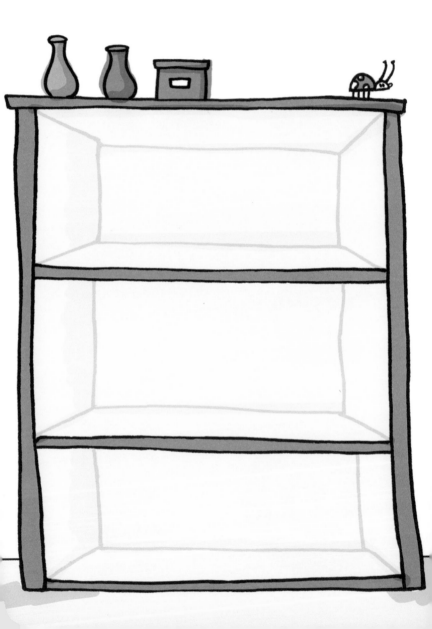

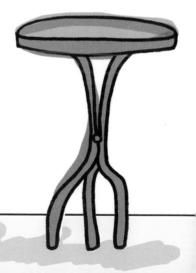

RISE AND SHINE!
Doodle faces on these garden friends.

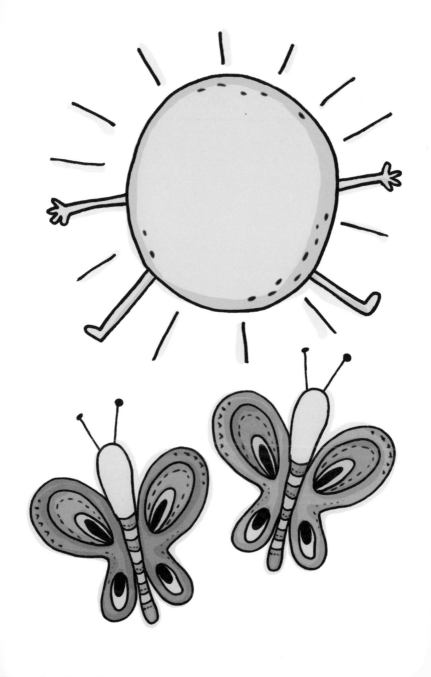

wall of doodles

GNARLY!
Doodle a skate park.

what's happening in town?
Finish the scene.

DOODLE FRAMES

Finish the patterns, and doodle inside the frames.

DOODLE POSTERS

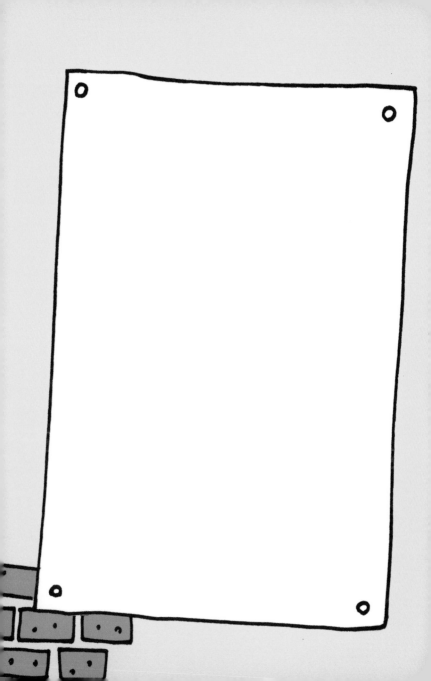

PLAY WITH YOUR FOOD!
Doodle faces on these lunch buddies.

Doodle a woodsy scene.

Vrrroom!
Add faces to these vehicles.

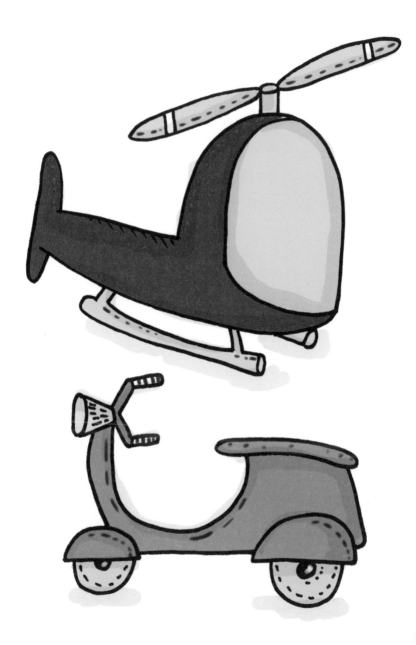

Doodle your family's portraits.

DOODLE SOMETHING

BUBBLY

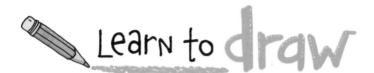

Learn to draw

Lion

Elephant

Finish the doodles by adding detail and color.

Doodle everything
you can think of that's...

DOODLE TEES!

My secret club

ROYAL DOODLES

PHOTO BOOTH

doodle something loopy.

Learn to draw

Turtle

Jellyfish

Finish the doodles by adding detail and color.

Doodle a place for these pets to play.

doodle yourself on the day you finish this book.

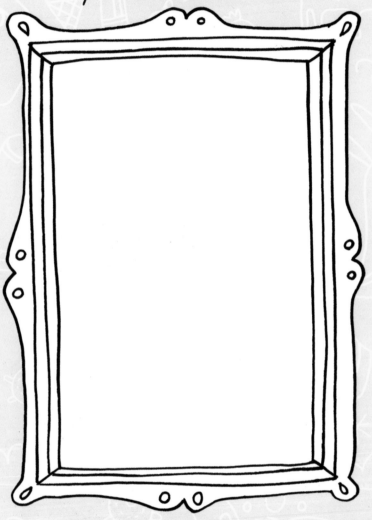

I finished this book on: _____